FARM ANIMALS

Turkeys

Faith Woodland

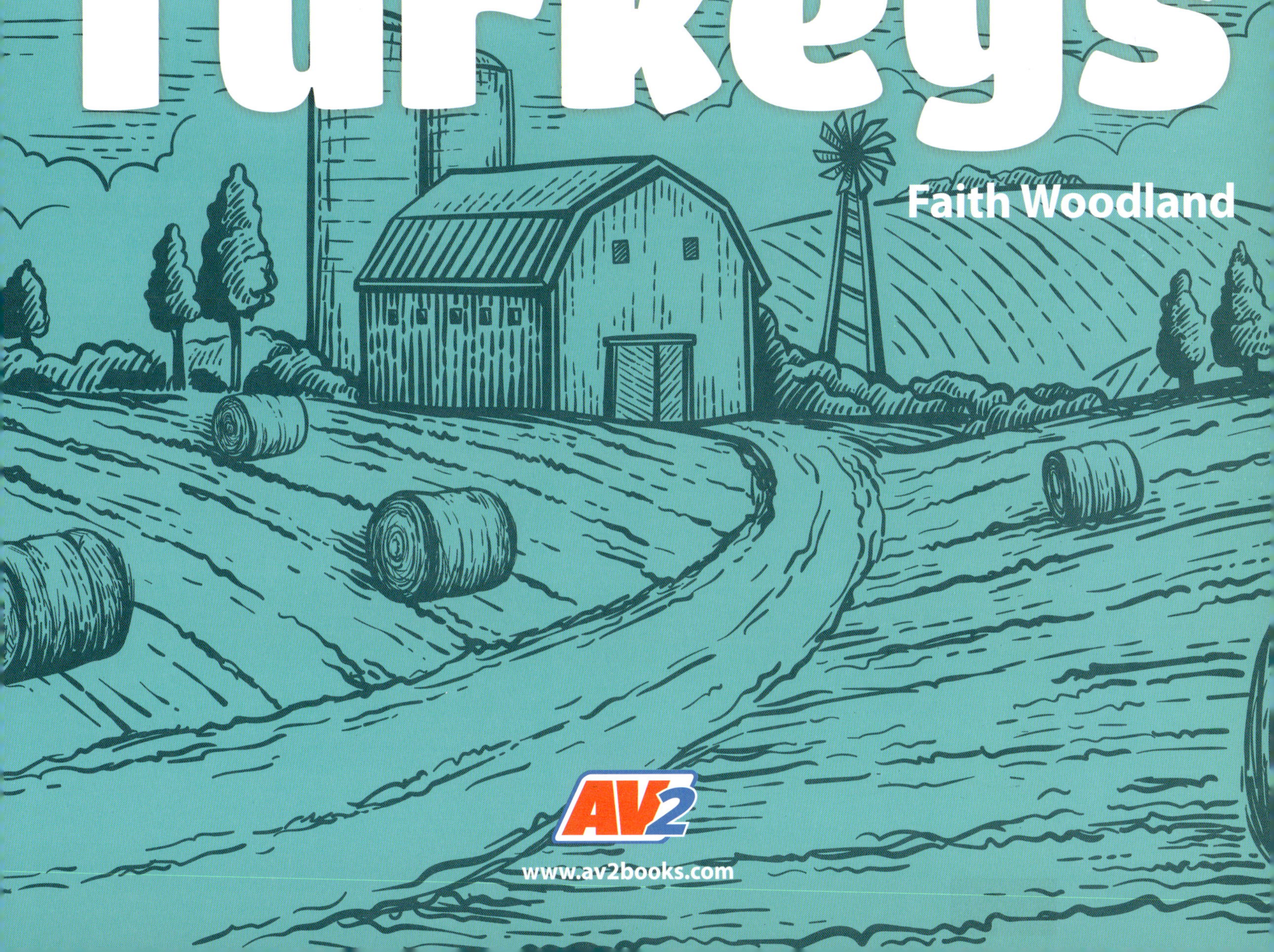

AV2
www.av2books.com

AV2

Step 1
Go to **www.av2books.com**

Step 2
Enter this unique code
DXZHGEDU2

Step 3
Explore your interactive eBook!

AV2 is optimized for use on any device

Your interactive eBook comes with...

Read

Audio
Listen to the entire book read aloud

Videos
Watch informative video clips

Weblinks
Gain additional information for research

Try This!
Complete activities and hands-on experiments

Key Words
Study vocabulary, and complete a matching word activity

Quizzes
Test your knowledge

Slideshows
View images and captions

View new titles and product videos at www.av2books.com

Turkeys

Contents

Tu

Turkeys are large birds that live on farms.

Farmers raise turkeys for meat.

keys

More turkeys are raised in Minnesota than in any other state.

A baby turkey is called a **poult**.

Poults hatch from eggs in the spring.

A turkey can lay up to **100 eggs**.

Mother turkeys look after their babies.

Poults need to stay warm and dry.

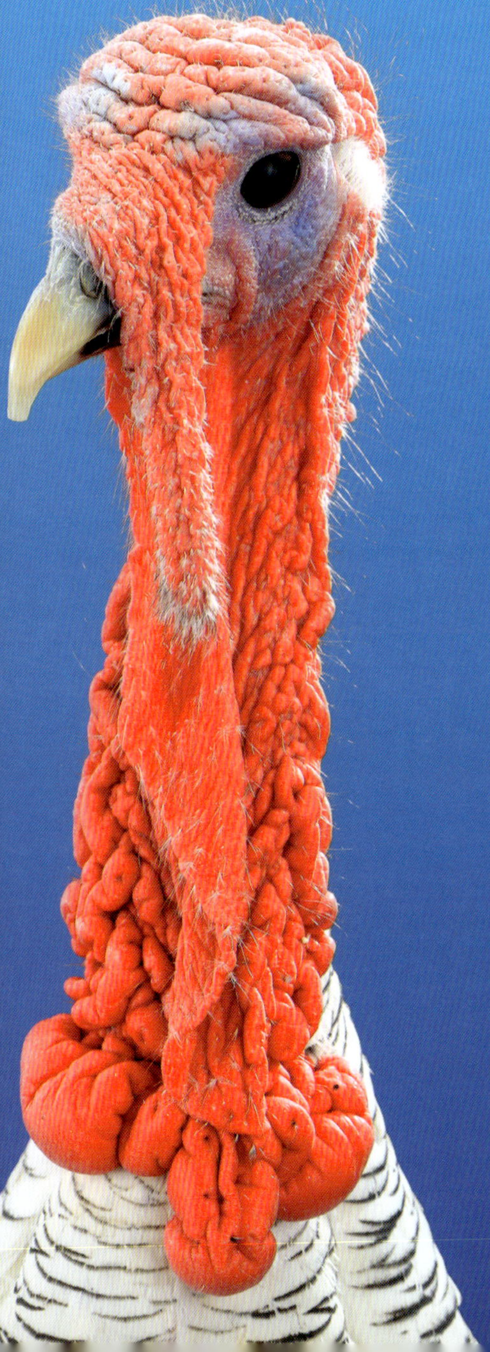

Turkeys are popular at Thanksgiving.

Some people call Thanksgiving "Turkey Day."

The **biggest** turkey **ever** weighed 86 pounds.

Turkeys eat insects and seeds.

Farmers feed turkeys grains to help them grow faster.

Turkeys make **gobbling** and **clucking** sounds.

They know each other by their voices.

Turkeys can make more than **20 different sounds**.

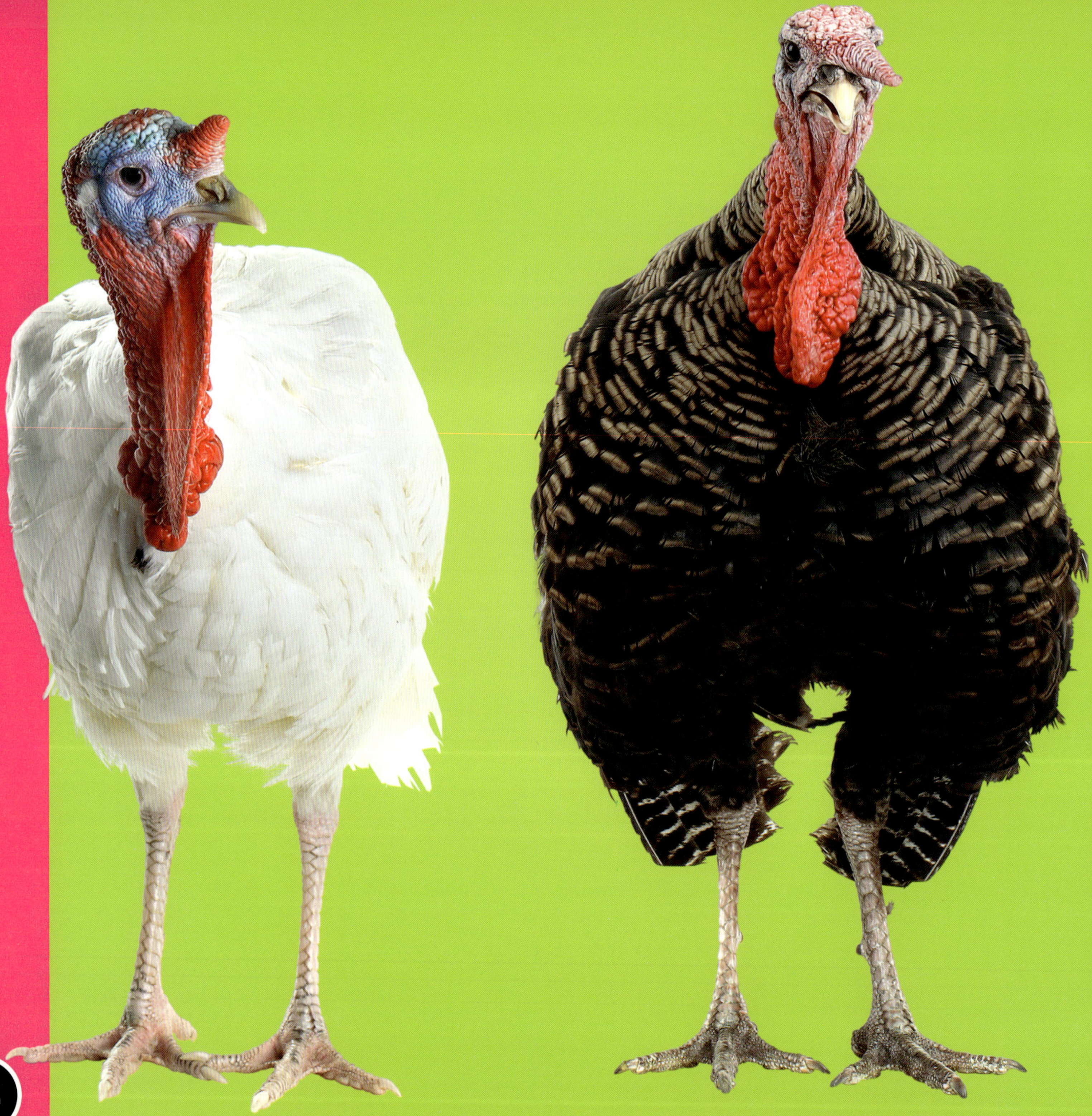

Male turkeys are called toms.

Female turkeys are called hens.

Toms have
colorful feathers.

They have skin
hanging from their
chin and forehead.

Turkeys need a clean, safe house.

They also need lots of exercise and fresh air.

TURKEY FACTS

These pages provide detailed information that expands on the interesting facts found in the book. They are intended to be used by adults as a learning support to help young readers round out their knowledge of each unique animal featured in the *Farm Animals* series and why it is kept and raised on farms.

Pages 4–5

Turkeys are large birds that live on farms. Turkeys are native to North America. Originally, domesticated turkeys were raised for their colorful feathers. Starting in the 1930s, they were raised for meat due to their large size and affordable cost. They are smart and naturally curious, easy to manage, and quick to raise.

Pages 6–7

A baby turkey is called a poult. Poults walk around as soon as they are hatched and are able to eat seeds and insects immediately. The babies need access to fresh, warm drinking water. They must be kept warm until their feathers grow in, which takes 6 to 8 weeks. Heat lamps can be used to keep the temperature at 100 degrees Fahrenheit (37.8 degrees Celsius) for the first two weeks. The temperature can be reduced by five degrees every week after.

Pages 8–9

Mother turkeys look after their babies. Female turkeys lay brownish, spotted eggs. They will lay the eggs in a shallow hole in the ground if they do not have a coop. Turkey eggs are not generally used for food, but instead are hatched and raised. The eggs hatch after 28 days of incubation. The mother turkey will guard her eggs from predators. A coop helps keep the eggs warm and protected from predators and the elements.

Pages 10–11

Turkeys are popular at Thanksgiving. It is not known if turkey was eaten at the first Thanksgiving feast, but it has become a main feature as the holiday has developed. One turkey provides enough meat for a large gathering of people. The meal becomes a feast with a few side dishes. Almost 250 million turkeys are raised in the United States each year.

Pages 12–13

Turkeys eat insects and seeds. In nature, turkeys are foragers, thriving in the woods where they eat insects, seeds, and acorns. Domesticated turkeys do well on a farm where they can forage through a garden and wander through woods as well. Turkeys benefit gardens as they eat harmful insects and fertilize the ground as they wander. Most farmers feed their turkeys corn and wheat to ensure that they grow quickly and are healthy for market.

Pages 14–15

Turkeys make gobbling and clucking sounds. Turkeys are extremely vocal. They make yelps, purrs, kee-kees, and gobbling sounds. They can recognize each other by the unique sounds each turkey makes. Male turkeys gobble to attract females and warn others about predators.

Pages 16–17

Male turkeys are called toms. A male turkey will grow to about 30 pounds (10 kilograms). A female grows to half that weight. As a group, turkeys are called a flock. The male puffs up his body, struts around, and spreads his feathers to attract females. While wild turkeys can fly and perch in trees, domesticated turkeys have lost the ability due to their higher weight. Despite their size, they can run up to 25 miles (40 kilometers) per hour.

Pages 18–19

Toms have colorful feathers. A turkey has 5,000 to 6,000 feathers covering its body. The feathers of the male can be red, purple, gold, and bronze. The hen is camouflaged in gray and brown feathers. The fleshy piece of skin dangling from the forehead is called a snood. The wattle is a piece of skin that hangs below the beak. The male also has spurs on his legs and a tuft of coarse black feathers called a beard growing from his breast.

Pages 20–21

Turkeys need a clean, safe house. Turkeys flourish on a farm where they get plenty of exercise and fresh air. They thrive in wooded areas but need to be protected from predators such as coyotes, foxes, weasels, and hawks. Turkeys need a clean, airy, roomy coop to keep them safe from predators, cold temperatures, and wet weather. Turkeys can get sick if their diet and living conditions are not properly cared for.

KEY WORDS

Research has shown that as much as 65 percent of all written material published in English is made up of 300 words. These 300 words cannot be taught using pictures or learned by sounding them out. They must be recognized by sight. This book contains 47 common sight words to help young readers improve their reading fluency and comprehension. This book also teaches young readers several important content words, such as proper nouns. These words are paired with pictures to aid in learning and improve understanding.

Page	Sight Words First Appearance
4	a, are, farms, for, large, live, on, that
5	any, in, more, other, state, than
7	can, is, the, to, up
8	after, look, mother, their
9	and, need
11	at, call, day, people, some
12	eat
13	grow, help, them
14	make, sounds
15	by, different, each, know, they
18	from, have
20	house
21	air, also, of

Page	Content Words First Appearance
4	birds, farmers, meat, turkeys
5	Minnesota
7	eggs, poult, spring
8	babies
9	dry, warm
11	Thanksgiving, Turkey Day
12	insects, seeds
13	grains
14	clucking, gobbling
15	voices
17	hens, toms
18	chin, feathers, forehead, skin
21	exercise

Published by AV2
350 5th Avenue, 59th Floor New York, NY 10118
Website: www.av2books.com

Library of Congress Cataloging-in-Publication Data

Names: Woodland, Faith, author.
Title: Turkeys / Faith Woodland.
Description: New York, NY : AV2, [2019] | Series: Farm animals | Audience: Grades 2-3 |
Identifiers: LCCN 2019040160 (print) | LCCN 2019040161 (ebook) | ISBN 9781791116446 (library binding) | ISBN 9781791116453 (paperback) | ISBN 9781791116460 (ebook other) | ISBN 9781791116477 (ebook other)
Subjects: LCSH: Turkeys--Juvenile literature. | Livestock--Juvenile literature.
Classification: LCC SF507 .W66 2019 (print) | LCC SF507 (ebook) | DDC 636.5/92--dc23
LC record available at https://lccn.loc.gov/2019040160
LC ebook record available at https://lccn.loc.gov/2019040161

Printed in Guangzhou, China
1 2 3 4 5 6 7 8 9 0 24 23 22 21 20

022020
100919

Art Director: Terry Paulhus Project Coordinators: Sara Cucini and Ryan Smith

AV2 acknowledges Shutterstock, iStock, and Minden as the primary image suppliers for this title.